Ron,

Thank you on behalf of all your colleagues over the years for your long and faithful service to the Division of Finance and to the FDIC.

Your work with delegations of authority and the DVS System and your workings with the Corporate Credit card were useful to the Division of Administration and many others within the Corporation.

I'll certainly miss your smiling face outside getting some fresh air as I come and go from the building — at almost any hour — even beyond the end of the normal duty day.

My best to you in all your future endeavors.

Fred Selby

Director
Division of Finance

SEPTEMBER, 2002

Beautiful America's

WASHINGTON, D.C.

Text by Tom Scanlan
Photography by Mae Scanlan

Revised Edition© 2002
Published by Beautiful America Publishing Company
2600 Progress Way
Woodburn, Oregon 97071

Library of Congress Cataloging in Publication Data
Beautiful America's Washington, D.C.
I. Washington (D.C.) — Description — 1981 — Views. 2. Washington Region —
Description and travel — Views. I. Scanlan, Mae Z. II. Title
F195.53   1988   917.53'044 — dc 19   88-1898
ISBN 0-89802-526-5
ISBN 0-89802-525-7 (paperback)

Lincoln Memorial

Abraham Lincoln

Contents

Washington, D.C.

My hometown Washington, the District of Columbia, the nation's capital, is one of the most fascinating and most beautiful big cities in the world. And that's not hometown bias. That's fact.

For a moment, try to forget the stunning Blue and Red and Green Rooms of the White House, the magnificent Capitol building with all its historic nooks and crannies, the incredible Library of Congress with all the knowledge it contains, all the monuments great and small, all the art indoors and outdoors, all the diverse and wondrous museums. Consider what must immediately delight the first-time visitor to Washington who arrives in spring or summer when most of the annual 20 million tourists come here: This big city is green!

Much of Washington is under an umbrella of trees and you won't find shadows from skyscrapers because skyscrapers are against the law. Washington also has a love affair with gardens.

In this strikingly different big city, Mother Nature has not been shoved aside for the grime of industry or the nitty-gritty of commerce. Yes, there is continual demand for more office space and new buildings keep replacing old ones. But trees, shrubs, flowers and grass continue to distinguish Washington as much as famous monuments, as much as its major "business," the federal government. By the late 1990s many of the trees were in bad shape, but early in the 21st century a wealthy widow donated a cool $50 million to plant new trees and repair old ones. This "Save the Trees" gift to the city kept Washington looking like Washington.

It is said there are more than 350,000 trees in Washington. Whoever is counting, such a count does not include Rock Creek Park which surely has millions of trees. Nor can it include hundreds of other parks throughout the city.

As for Rock Creek, how many cities have an uncorrupted urban wilderness of nearly 1,800 acres in its midst? Rock Creek has horse stables and bridle paths (General George Catlett Marshall was riding there one Sunday morning when the Japanese bombed Pearl Harbor), picnic areas, many miles of bike and hiking trails, and the 168-acre National Zoo. At this zoo, birds fly high in "The Great Outdoors Flight Cage" where there are no barriers between man and bird. Acrobatic sea lions and more than 2,500 other animals, including famous bears and pandas, also reside here. There is no admission charge.

At last count, there are more than 750 other smaller parks in the city. And thanks in large measure to how the city was laid out by Pierre Charles L'Enfant in 1791, with wide avenues reaching huge circles, with plazas and the famous Mall (even bigger than L'Enfant planned), there are countless other smaller spaces for grass and blooming plants.

Visitors should somehow find time for a stroll through the gardens at Dumbarton Oaks in Georgetown. Though near busy Wisconsin Avenue, you seem miles away from traffic on these 10 acres of formal and informal gardens, terraces, fountains and reflecting pools. Tourists weary from trooping through crowded museums on the Mall are also advised to relax in the uncrowded United States Botanic Garden, on the Mall near

Thomas Jefferson

8

Jefferson Memorial

the Capitol. This garden, actually a glass building, has more than 500 varieties of orchids and thousands of tropical plants. It was extensively remodeled and enlarged in 2001.

Tourists jam the city for two weeks of cherry blossom time in early spring, Lady Bird Johnson made certain there is no lack of daffodils in unexpected places, and there are thousands (millions?) of tulips seemingly everywhere in late spring (including about 250,000 of these Dutch beauties beside the Tidal Basin). But Washington — as a city — was a late bloomer with severe growing pains. For decades, Washington meant mud and mosquitoes, politics and pestilence. Only politics is still with us.

In The Beginning, Swampland

Much of the city was built on swampland. Though Washington was created 70 years before the Civil War, North-South squabbling had much to do with its very existence. Southern congressmen didn't want the nation's capital to be permanently in Philadelphia, where dwelt abolitionist Quakers, and northern congressmen didn't want "the federal city" in a slave-holding state. Alexander Hamilton and other wise men sought compromise and a close congressional vote set the general location beside the Potomac River, far from the madding crowd, with land to come from Maryland and Virginia. President Washington was given the job of choosing the exact sight of the 100-mile square capital city to-be. (It is 68 square miles now, mainly because that part of the city west of the Potomac wasn't needed in the 1840's and was returned to Virginia at Virginia's request.)

Washington chose an area beside Georgetown, a major tobacco port in the mid-1750's. (Georgetown University became the first Catholic university in the United States in 1789.) Washington also chose L'Enfant, a French engineer who had fought with American troops during the revolution, to design the city.

L'Enfant did so in a big way. He decided Jenkins Hill (now Capital Hill or simply "the Hill" to Washingtonians) was the perfect site for the Capitol building and placed the "president's house" on flat, low ground about a mile away. He used two old existing roads that met at Jenkins Hill and added what he hoped would be colossal avenues coming from the Hill to bisect rectangular squares of streets. The avenues were to avoid monotony and to enable people to reach central parts of the city by the shortest routes. The Mall or "public walk," which now runs two miles from the Capitol to the Lincoln Memorial with the Washington Monument in between, was incorporated into L'Enfant's plan from a sketch by Jefferson. Three commissioners who headed the project are credited with naming the streets alphabetically one way and numerically the other way, which still helps visitors today.

Constant, bitter legal battles by L'Enfant with property owners, real estate speculators and the commissioners forced Washington to fire the headstrong, imaginative L'Enfant — reluctantly, historians claim — after the Frenchman was on the job for only about one year. L'Enfant grumbled about the butchering of his master plan, but his dreams for a city unlike any other did, eventually, come true. From his grave in Arlington National Cemetery, there is a good view of the city and his ghost must be pleased.

In 1800, President John Adams and wife Abigail moved into the new White House (Abigail hung her wash out to dry in the unfinished East Room) and federal government workers — all 131 of them — came from Philadelphia to the new federal city named Washington by Congress. Later that year, with one section of the Capitol building completed, Congress met here for the first time.

And what they all discovered in this so-called city were unpaved, unbricked, uncobblestoned roads, disease, a housing shortage and Washington's famous summer humidity. (About Washington weather: usually seasonal but sometimes there are summer days in May or spring days in late June. Winters can be mild or rugged with

United States Capitol

Inside Rotunda

considerable snow. And bank on July and August to be hot and humid although experts contend that Washington is no more humid than most big U.S. cities. They say it's the combination of high temperatures and moderate humidity that makes some days so unpleasant.)

In 1800, there were only a half-dozen buildings along hazardous, muddy, or dusty Pennsylvania Avenue and many said the federal city should be nearly anywhere but here. Washington also lacked — and this is an understatement — the sophistication of Philadelphia, Boston, or Charleston. Nearly two-thirds of the Washington-Alexandria-Georgetown 1800 population of 14,000 were slaves and white illiterates. French visitor La Rouchefoucauld, a famous wit, wasn't merely joking when he suggested that the city might never "be capable of growing to a point that could make it a bearable place for those fated to live in it."

'Boss' Changed the City

By 1814, Congress was only nine votes short of abandoning the city after the British torched the White House, the Capitol and the Library of Congress, including Jefferson's book collection that got the library started.

Even by 1860, when Abraham Lincoln became president and when slaves were still auctioned a block away from the White House, Pennsylvania Avenue was a municipal sewer. And the Mall was no delightful "public walk" as envisioned by Jefferson. Only wild pigs and sheep strolled beside the 1848 cornerstone of an ignored, fundless, only partially completed Washington Monument, with smelly slaughterhouses nearby.

Washington did not begin to become a decent place to live until the 1870's, thanks to a controversial city boss, Alexander Sheperd, a friend of President Grant and the city's second and last governor. Aptly nicknamed "Boss," Shepherd laid hundreds of miles of sidewalk, planted 50,000 trees, extended water lines and gas mains, demolished and rebuilt private property as he saw fit, graded 118 miles of roads, filled in the malarial Washington Canal which too often overflowed into Pennsylvania Avenue, and put asphalt on that "Grand Avenue," as L'Enfant had called it.

Boss Shepherd also put the city in debt. Though Grant wanted to keep him on the job, Congress wanted no part of him or any governor with such power. Shepherd declared bankruptcy and took off for Mexico. In Mexico the impoverished Shepherd discovered silver and gold in a defunct mine and became a millionaire.

14

In many sections of the city a visitor may notice that unlike Philadelphia, Baltimore or New York, there are gardens or grass in front of row houses. This is because the streets were extremely wide to begin with and when they were paved during Boss Shepherd's reign even this big spender realized that there was not enough money to pave entire streets. So half the width of streets was set aside for unpaved "parking." And homeowners were permitted to fence or enclose all of the unneeded "parking" space in front of their houses. Thus each house could have about 20 feet of garden in front on public property. (You know you're in Georgetown when you see no front yards. Georgetown of course preceded Washington and was not involved in the city's paving problems.) The unusual width of D.C. streets was also the reason why trees that would become huge were planted to line the streets. This also helped to make Washington look much different from other U.S. cities in the 19th century and — indeed — now.

The next period of major city change came during President Franklin D. Roosevelt's "New Deal" days in the 1930's and the World War II years that followed. As the federal government became larger and larger with more and more agencies created, huge federal buildings went up. Thus the "Federal Triangle" of mammoth buildings from 14th to 6th Streets, northwest, between Pennsylvania and Constitution Avenues, including the headquarters of your beloved Internal Revenue Service. World War II added the Pentagon, with its 17.5 miles of corridors, across the Potomac in Virginia.

The war turned what some — notably New Yorkers — kept calling "basically a sleepy southern town" into a busy metropolis. And during the 1950's and 1960's there was much highway building and slum clearance, especially in southwest Washington where Al Jolson grew up. Many poor families were forced into overcrowded areas elsewhere in the city as large new federal buildings and townhouses replaced the brick rowhouses of southwest. This massive redevelopment project also destroyed picturesque restaurants on the waterfront, which is cleaner and neater looking now but lacks the character and charisma of what used to be. Even the waterfront's fish market looks almost antiseptic.

For the past 30 years or so, Washington has become surrounded by more and more suburbs and isolated housing developments in Virginia and Maryland further and further away from the city itself. What used to be countryside near Washington can now be clogged with traffic on suburban main drags. And Crystal City and Rosslyn, in Virginia beside the Potomac and linked by eye to Washington, boast new tall buildings that defy Washington's building height tradition. In similar fashion, Bethesda, in Maryland, suddenly became a business, restaurant and hotel center in the late 1980's, complete with fancy and sometimes ugly new buildings to rival those in Crystal City.

For those of us who live in the city, many visitors are startled to discover how close downtown is to residential areas. Many Washingtonians with lovely backyard gardens are only five or ten minutes from the White House. In this regard, Washington is not like New York or Philadelphia. I live in the Chevy Chase area near the Maryland line amidst tall old trees, a variety of birds and a few raccoons. And it takes only 20 minutes to get downtown by car.

Washington Monument

Westfront, United States Capitol

Bronze of F.D.R., by Neil Estern, F.D.R. Memorial

THEY (WHO) SEEK TO ESTABLISH
SYSTEMS OF GOVERNMENT BASED ON
THE REGIMENTATION OF ALL HUMAN
BEINGS BY A HANDFUL OF INDIVIDUAL
RULERS... CALL THIS A NEW ORDER.
IT IS NOT NEW AND IT IS NOT ORDER.

F.D.R. and Fala, F.D.R. Memorial

Urban Bread Line, F.D.R. Memorial

Unknown U.S. Soldier

Arlington National Cemetery

Tomb of the Unknown Soldier

Washinton Monument

(Following pages) United States Capitol

The White House

The Executive Office Building

Library of Congress

American Red Cross Building

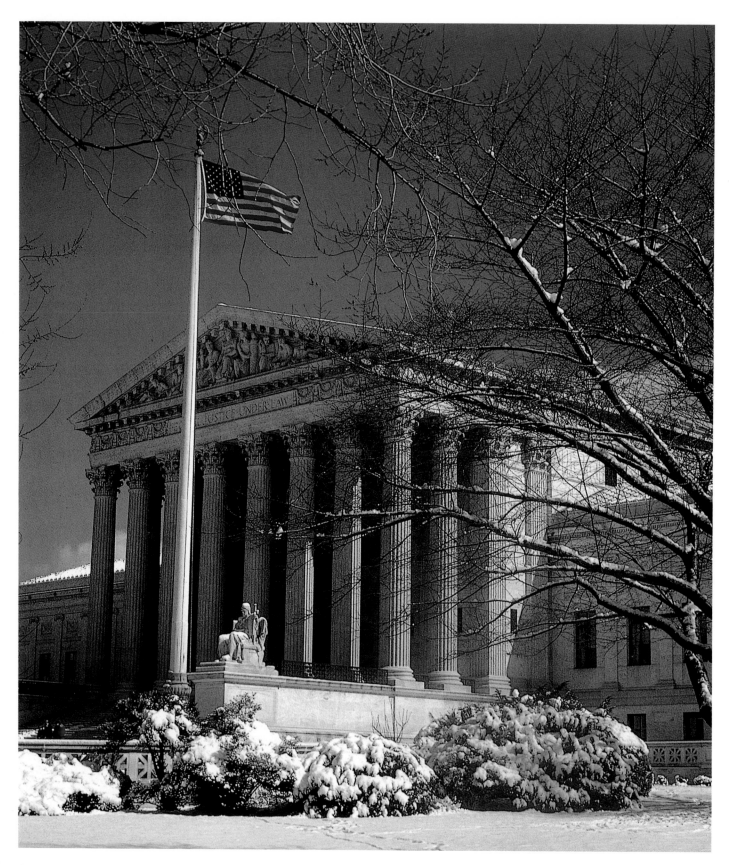

Supreme Court Building

Museum of Natural History

Reagan Building

Taxation Without Representation

The city's biggest employer is the federal government but most Washingtonians do not work for the federal government. And those of us who live in Washington remain the only residents of a capital city in a democracy in the world who have no voting representatives. There is one D.C. representative in Congress but this House deligate can vote only in committee, not on the House floor, and there is no D.C. senator. Wyoming, Alaska, and the Dakotas, all states with populations comparable to D.C., each have one seat in the House of Representatives and two Senate seats. "No taxation without representation" remains a meaningful argument for Washingtonians who pay stiff city taxes as well as federal taxes.

There is not a tourist's Washington and a Washingtonian's Washington. Washingtonians enjoy their city. Those joggers you see beside the Potomac are not tourists. Nor are the sunbathers behind the Kennedy Center and the volleyball and soft-ball players nearby. Locals, as well as visitors, go paddle boating in the Tidal Basin. Those who live here also congregate for free military, big band or bluegrass concerts beside the Jefferson Memorial, the Capitol, Air and Space Museum, and the Washington Monument. Washingtonians also crowd auditoriums where musical, historical, literary and scientific programs are produced by the Smithsonian Institution, the Library of Congress and many other federal and private organizations.

The grim, tragic realities of contemporary big city life are undeniably present in Washington. This includes crime inspired by expensive narcotics "habits" and insufficient jail space.

The D.C. metropolitan area, with a population of more than 3,600,000, is predominately white, but the city itself, with 572,000 (according to the 2000 census) is predominately black. That census also revealed that the city's racial and ethic makeup is changing, with blacks moving out (many to Prince George's County in Maryland) and Asians and Hispanics moving in. Also, many whites, tired of heavy beltway traffic commuting to work in the city, are moving back into Washington. The majority black population figure, 66 percent in 1990, was down to 60 percent in 2000. Because decent apartment and home prices keep going up, some contend — with good reason — that the city is in danger of becoming a city of two classes: the affluent class, made up of whites and blacks, and the welfare class, mostly black. Predominately black areas in southeast (Anacostia), northeast and that part of northwest east of Rock Creek Park scarred by riots following the murder of Rev. Martin Luther King, Jr. in 1968, make up the Washington that most tourists and many suburbanites never see.

Because of crime, inferior public schools, and the failure of a bloated city bureaucracy to provide decent services to its taxpayers (the city excels in issuing parking tickets come snow or come shine, but potholes are common and snow removal is uncommon), many thousands of middle class residents, black and white, have moved to nearby Maryland and Virginia in recent years. Newcomers keep coming but the city's population has been going down for decades. In 1970, 757,000 lived in the District, about 200,000 more than in 1996. This continual drop in population plays havoc with the city's tax base, and the mayor, the city council, and Congress have done little to help. It's been much talk, no action, for many years.

As for crime, tourists are advised that what is sometimes called "the monumental core" of the city, where the major tourist attractions are, is not a crime center. But visitors are asking for serious trouble if they explore certain other city areas, especially at night. Any city resident, white or black, can tell you where those areas are. During the daytime, "the monumental core" is as safe, maybe safer, than downtown areas in most other major U. S. cities.

Despite a large number on welfare, a recent study showed the D.C. metropolitan area is far and away the most affluent in the nation. This report showed that income was 42 percent above the average of all U.S. households and 11 percent higher than the second-ranked metropolitan area of San Francisco-Oakland. The D.C. area first gained the rank of most affluent with the 1970 census and has been increasing its lead ever since. Washington also has more college graduates than any other metropolitan area, with about one third of its residents holding a college degree.

The city's fiscal health has vastly improved since the days of Mayor Marion Barry. As is true of big major cities in the U. S., major crime is down but there is still too much crime fueled by crack cocaine and too many uninsured people. Some middle-class families are returning to the city and improving downtrodden neighborhoods, but school system problems remain serious.

Navy and Marine Memorial

"Arts of Peace" bronzes at Lincoln Memorial Circle

Downtown is Coming Back!

Despite common big city ills, Washington keeps getting better in many ways. Major league baseball has not returned (an absurdity in this city where Walter Johnson, Goose Goslin and Josh Gibson were heroes) but the once-filthy Potomac is fairly clean now, Pennsylvania Avenue has improved dramatically, and downtown is coming back.

The city's $100 million convention center, opened in 1983, sparked redevelopment in the old downtown area, and early in the 21st century a much larger convention center is going up across from the first convention center. As downtown outdoor parking lots decrease and new buildings go up, preservationists have helped to preserve the character of older buildings needing repair, thus downtown Washington is not beginning to look like Bethsda, and other collections of dull, predictable office buildings in nearby Maryland and Virginia. The city's major sports team, with many devout fans, the Washington Redskins, left the city for a new football stadium in Landover, Maryland, more than 15 miles from the heart of Washington. As has been true for decades, season ticket-holders have the seats. The city's pro basketball team went the other way, moving from Maryland to the new MCI Center sports arena in downtown Washington. (The team also changed its nickname from "Bullets" to "Wizards" because the former name was a reminder of the city's crime problem.) The more successful National Hockey League team, the Capitals (or "Caps") also play in this new downtown arena (beside a Metro subway stop) that has enlivened the city's Chinatown area.

Pennsylvania Avenue has new parks, new hotels and office buildings, 700 more trees and many more benches. The Old Post Office building with its 315-foot tower, making it the second highest building in the city (yes, the Washington Monument is number one) was not only saved from demolition but remodeled extensively. A trip to the tower for the view is recommended.

The city's famous "hotel of presidents," The Willard, was also saved from destruction and restored to Gilded Age opulence. Stroll its famous block-long "Peacock Alley" and recall that this was where the nation's VIPs began to strut their stuff when Teddy Roosevelt became president in 1901. (An earlier hotel on this corner of Pennsylvania Avenue and 14th Street, called Willard's, was where presidents met the press who worked across the street on "newspaper row," where the National Press Club is now. Julia Ward Howe wrote "The Battle Hymn of the Republic" at Willard's in 1861.) In front of the Willard there are iceskaters in wintertime. And the new Western Plaza, catty-cornered from the Willard, has a good-sized pond with ducks plus lots of walking room. Under your feet you will find a map of the area, a diagram of the White House and provocative quotations. A block away, beneath one of the city's large new hotels–the J.W. Mariott –The Shops at National Place offer a variety of goods, trinkets, food.

The famous Mayflower Hotel on Connecticut Avenue, where President Coolidge's Inaugural Ball was held in 1925 a month after the hotel opened, has been spruced up in a major way. And in Washington's West End area, between downtown and Georgetown, there are first-class hotels in this once dreary area. There are many good new restaurants downtown, and marble-floored Union Station, opened in 1907 as the largest train station in the world, was extensively remodeled during the late 1980s and now includes numerous shops and popular food places as well as one first-class restaurant. There is also a huge new federal building downtown beside Pennsylvania Avenue. This is known as the Reagan Building and is officially the Ronald Reagan Building and International Trade Center.

The so-called World War I "tempos" (temporary buildings for the Army and Navy on Constitution Avenue) in permanent use for decades, are long gone, replaced by still more parkland and the compelling Vietnam Veterans Memorial with its unforgettable black granite walls inscribed with the names of more than 58,000 dead and missing in action.

Twenty years ago, Washington was considered a second-rate restaurant town. Not now. But many out-of-towners will suggest that restaurants described as "expensive" in guidebooks might more properly be termed very expensive. Nor is booze by the drink cheap. Yet Washington is said to consume more liquor per capita than any other city in the nation. There are many parties, business lunches, and lobbyists in this city.

The Kennedy Center for Performing Arts, overlooking the Potomac near the famed Watergate apartment-office-hotel complex, has brought major theater to Washington as never before. The Center has a 2,750-seat concert hall, an opera house, and a more intimate theater, the Eisenhower. A grand foyer with crystal chandeliers and a seven-foot-high bronze bust of President Kennedy opens to a large terrace overlooking the Potomac. Great view, particularly at night when you see the many lights of newly-developed Washington Harbor in Georgetown.

The city's National Symphony Orchestra may not be one of the world's greatest but it is infinitely superior to what it was 30 years ago. There is also a variety of night life with few sleazy joints extant downtown. These were once common. Forty years ago strip clubs and prostitution shops posing as massage or photo parlors were in business only four blocks from the White House. Twenty new office buildings have replaced clubs peddling flesh and pornography in this Franklin Square neighborhood.

Duke Ellington's hometown still has many fine jazz musicians but their "gigs" are not always advertised and you may have to ask people who know about such music to discover where to find it. The famous Howard Theater, where I was among those who thrilled to the artistry of the great black swing bands in the late 1930's and early 1940's, still stands but is tragically dark, perhaps forever. This 7th and Florida Avenue area, once a center of black night life, along with the similar 14th and U Street area, has gone downhill, although the old Lincoln Theater has been remodeled and opened again after decades of darkness.

Older Washingtonians well remember when this city was firmly segregated. Like other white youngsters involved with jazz in the 30's and 40's, I was welcome to see Count Basie or Jimmie Lunceford at the Howard, but blacks were not permitted to enjoy Teddy Wilson and Lionel Hampton creating great music with Benny Goodman at the Earle theater downtown. Indeed, blacks could not go to any white theater and about the only white restaurant that would serve them was the one in Union Station. It was worse than Virginia where blacks were permitted in some white movie theater balconies. This all began to change in the late 1940's before famous lunch counter sit-ins in the South. And with integration, many would-be top Howard University students went to white colleges instead. Similarly, academically superior Dunbar High School, which

Mount Vernon

produced so many of the nation's foremost black scholars and famous people, became just another city school.

In recent years, the big change in Washington has been underground. It is now much easier to get around town thanks to our subway. Tourists should forget taxis. Cabs are moving from a confusing zone system to a meter system and this may stop overcharging incidents. Use the clean, fast subway system known as — what else? — the Metro. Not all of the system is underground. About 40 percent, mainly in Maryland and Virginia, is outdoors. Metro stops are identified by "M" signs and escalators take you underground. A farecard system works okay (longer rides and rush-hour rides cost more) and this Metro is not to be confused with the New York subway system. There is a crime-free atmosphere. Stations, spacious with arched ceilings, are air-conditioned and monitored by internal television. There is no smoking. And, to thwart crime, no lavatories. The Metro does not go to Mount Vernon, does not stop directly in Georgetown, but it does go to National Airport (extensively remodeled, expanded, and officially renamed Ronald Reagan Washington National Airport in 1998, but still called National Airport by most Washingtonians) and Alexandria, an interesting historic town tourists are wise to visit.

But the Metro has not solved rush-hour traffic jams. And the beltway around the city is becoming more crowded every year. If you must bring still another car to Washington, remember that metered spaces are not easy to find and parking lots are expensive. As for parking on streets downtown, that is usually—trust me—almost impossible.

You Can't Be Bored

It takes months, maybe years, to see all that ought to be seen in Washington. But whatever your interests may be, Washington has something for you. You can't be bored in Washington. Let's begin with some of the major sights:

If you have time to visit only one building, my vote is the United States Capitol. This magnificent building is where American history has happened, is happening, and will happen. Take the tour that leaves every 15 minutes from the Rotunda (under the dome). See the House or Senate in session (if you're not on tour, get a pass from your senator or congressman's office). And try to watch a congressional hearing in nearby Senate and House office buildings. Check the Washington Post's "Today in Congress" box in the morning to see what hearings are to take place. Many are not crowded and the more obscure ones might deal with subject matter right up your alley.

From the ten-ton bronze doors on the east side of the building to the old Senate and Supreme Court chambers in the north wing, history is everywhere. As you peer into the old Senate chambers, envision in your mind's eye Daniel Webster, Henry Clay or John Calhoun delivering a rip-roaring speech.

You may want to lunch in the Senate or House cafeterias, where prices are reasonable, or ride the Senate subway which goes from the basements of the Senate office buildings to the Capitol (no charge on this subway). Or take a look at the Caucus Room on the second floor of the Old Senate (or Russell) Office Building, where the Army-McCarthy, Watergate and Iran-Contra hearings were held.

The Supreme Court, the Library of Congress, and the Folger Shakespearean Library are all nearby. If the high court is in session, you must be early to have any chance of watching because there are only about 100 seats for the public. But you can walk around the first floor and the ground floor on your own and there is a 30-minute film telling you what the court is all about.

The Library of Congress is the largest library in the world with more than 75 million items (books, maps, newspapers, music, tapes, photos). Its three buildings have more than 320 miles of shelves. Anyone can order a book (most card files have been replaced by computers) but you will have to wait for delivery. In addition to many rare books (including pre-1500 volumes and Hitler's personal library), the world's largest library even has 30,000 recordings on cylinders that predate phonograph records. Don't miss the Main Reading Room in the old Jefferson building, under the dome. This 19th-century structure in the Italian Renaissance style has weathered criticism for being "Victorian Rococo" and remains one of the city's marvelous sights, outside and inside with great archways and elaborate ornamentation. A Gutenberg Bible is on display. The Folger Library, two blocks away, includes an Elizabethan theater in use between May and October. Notice the bas-relief panels, on the outside, that depict scenes from Shakespeare's plays. Scholars studying here pause for tea with staff every afternoon.

The Most Popular Museum

The Mall is where tourists congregate (subway riders use the Smithsonian stop, Mall exit). It extends two miles from the Capitol to the Lincoln Memorial with the Washington Monument near the center.

The most popular museum on the Mall, indeed the most popular tourist attraction in the city (including the White House and the Capitol), is the National Air and Space Museum, opened in 1976. Ten million visitors come here every year and can any other museum in the world match that?

This Smithsonian museum has 240 aircraft, assorted missiles and rockets, a planetarium, movies on a five-story screen, the Wright Brothers' Kitty Hawk Flyer, Lindbergh's Spirit of St. Louis, John Glenn's Friendship 7, and the Apollo 11 command module. Visitors like to touch the moon rocks.

Two blocks away is the Hirshhorn Museum and Sculpture Garden, known as "the doughnut on the Mall." See it and you'll know why. Rodin's The Burghers of Calais and some marvelous small figures by Daumier are among the 6,500 pieces in the Hirshhorn's permanent collection.

Nearby, past the original Smithsonian building, in distinctive red sandstone and called "The Castle" for apparent reason, discover the peaceful, uncrowded Freer Gallery of Art, a treasure house of jade sculpture, other Oriental art, and the world's

"The Castle", Smithsonian Institution

Display in Air and Space Museum

largest collection of Whistler's work.

Another of the newer museums draws many tourists. This is the U.S. Holocaust Memorial Museum, located south of the Mall, two blocks from the Washington Monument. It contains countless true horrors in War II Germany and a library with 20,000 volumes detailing evil. This is across the street from one of the mammoth Department of Agriculture buildings — who says Washington is not involved with farmers?

The murder of one great American is delineated in the Lincoln Museum on 10th Street, where Lincoln died following his assassination across the street at Ford's Theatre. The museum has the clothes he wore that night and the derringer used to kill him. Ford's Theatre has been restored to look as it did in Lincoln's time and once again has live stage productions.

For those interested in money, the nation's largest money-printing plant at the Bureau of Engraving and Printing has a 20-minute self-guided tour. This is at 14th and C Streets, southwest, a block south of the Mall. Lines are sometimes long.

Five Rooms at the White House

Most all visitors to the 132-room White House normally see only five rooms. On an average day about 6,000 take the tour. You'll get a peek at the Jacqueline Kennedy Rose Garden on the way to the East Room, used for press conferences, parties and concerts. The more formal Blue Room, the Red Room with priceless antiques, the Green Room, and the State Dining Room are also on the tour. You won't see the Oval Office which is smaller than you might expect. Many assistant secretaries of federal departments have much larger offices. And be aware that visitors are rushed through the White House in the spring and summer, in usually ten to 15 minutes. But however long the wait, most everyone agrees it's time well spent. In 1995 because of terrorist activity elsewhere, not in Washington, Pennsylvania Avenue from 15th to 17th, in front of the White House, was closed off to auto and bus traffic. But there is even more room to walk by now. The closing of this part of Pennsylvania Avenue–despite the iron fence in front of the White House and the distance between the President's home and the fence–created traffic problems and, at this writing, many Washingtonians continue to campaign for the street to be opened for cars as well as pedestrians again Guess what? A commission is studying the matter.

Other museums on the Mall: The National Museum of American History (including a Victorian ice cream parlor and gowns worn by all the First Ladies), Natural History (including an "insect zoo" with working beehive), and the National Gallery of Art (many Washingtonians still call it "the Mellon" for it's founder Andrew Mellon). This is unquestionably one of the great art museums. The main, or West Building, has works by Raphael, da Vinci, Titian, Degas, Renoir, Monet and many other great painters. The newer East Building, opened in 1978, is the site of major exhibits and is probably the best example of modern architecture (by I.M. Pei) in the city. And in 1987, two unusual underground museums opened in front of the Smithsonian Castle. The

Arthur M. Sackler Gallery concentrates on Asian art and includes bronze vessels and jade carvings thousands of years old. The Museum of African Art has fascinating terra cotta and ivory sculpture.

There's a great view of the city from the top of the Washington Monument, reached by elevator. Like many other kids years ago, I walked up the 898 steps but no one is allowed to do that now. But you can walk down. The monument's walls are 15 feet thick at the bottom and 16 inches thick at the top. Lines are often long but seem to move rapidly. On July 4th, the Mall is jammed with a half million visitors and locals watching fireworks zoom around the monument. For those with tripods, it's a great photo opportunity.

The Mall

There are 357 National Park Service sites in the nation. The oldest is Yellowstone, the largest is in Alaska, and the one with the most people walking on it, per square mile, must be the Mall in Washington.

There are occasional days when hundreds of thousands of people are trampling on the Mall, celebrating or protesting something, but most of the time there is plenty of room to stroll up and down the Mall (it's about two miles from the Capitol Building to the Lincoln Memorial) while choosing which fascinating museum along the way to enjoy during your visit.

And no matter what your area of enthusiasm, expertise, or causal interest, there will be something to excite you on or beside the Mall. There is major, and rare, American, European, African, Near Eastern and Oriental art. There are museums devoted to American history, natural history, sculpture, air and space. You can find Chinese jade 3,000 years old (in Sackler Gallery) or orchids inside a glass building. Mall beauty includes a four-acre garden with old-fashioned Victorian flower beds and English teak benches.

The Mall is now more or less the way L'Enfant planned in 1791. But much of it was a cattle pasture in the 19th century, and even by 1907 the Mall featured huge piles of coal beside a railroad station (where President Garfield was assassinated, and where the National Gallery of Art now stands).

Until 1971, large "temporary" World War I office buildings for the Army and the Navy were on the west end of the Mall. Now there is a park and the Vietnam Veterans "wall." At any time of the day you will see people searching for particular names.

In the spring and summer months, there are many free concerts at noon and in the evening on the Mall. The Mall also hosts an American folk festival in the summer and many other special events, scheduled and unscheduled. And at night, at the west

Inside National Geographic Building

Inside Union Station

National Museum of African Art, Smithsonian Grounds

end of the Mall, under soft floodlights, there is the inspiring, unforgettable sight of Daniel Chester French's majestic statue of Lincoln, facing toward the Washington Monument, and beyond to the Capitol.

It may be an apocryphal story, but "they say" it really happened. A woman got off the Metro subway at the Smithsonian stop, came up the escalator, looked up and down the Mall, and asked a nearby policeman: "So, if this is the Mall, where are all the stores?"

"Lady," he replied, "it's not that kind of mall."

Right. In fact, it's a mall unlike any other mall in the world.

Lafayette Park, across from the White House, is popular with pigeons, brown-baggers, and pickets. (And that's not Lafayette on horseback in the center. That's Andrew Jackson. Lafayette is in the park's southeast corner.) The restored Decatur House is one of the Federal-style townhouses facing the square and is worthy of your time. Commissioned by Naval hero Stephen Decatur, who lived here less than a year before meeting death in a duel, it was also the home for Henry Clay and Martin Van Buren.

The Lincoln Memorial is unforgettable at any time but particularly compelling at night when the memorial is reflected in the rectangular pool below. Two rows of Ionic columns flank Daniel Chester French's 19-foot marble statue. Behind the columns are inscribed Lincoln's Second Inaugural Address ("with malice toward none, with charity for all. . .") and the Gettysburg Address ("government of the people, by the people, for the people. . ."). Walk around this temple-like classic Greek memorial, beside the 36 Doric columns, for a view of the Potomac River, Memorial Bridge and Arlington National Cemetery across the Potomac.

Choice of this site for the memorial was controversial in 1912. Powerful Speaker of the House "Uncle Joe" Cannon swore he would "never let a memorial to Abraham Lincoln be erected in that damned swamp." But Uncle Joe lost this one. In what had once been desolate swampland, the memorial was completed in 1922. There is no subway stop near the Lincoln Memorial and don't try to drive here during rush hours unless you want to wind up in Virginia.

The reflecting pool is a great "photo-op" for those with cameras and is understandably popular with visitors, including many sea gulls and some ducks. It is 2,000 feet long, thirty inches deep, and holds seven million gallons of water.

Nearby is the compelling "Wall of Names" (designed by Maya Ying Lin) at the Vietnam Veterans Memorial, listing more than 58,000 killed and missing in that war. Every day rubbings of the names in black granite (from India) are taken by loved ones. Every day mementos are left beside the wall. The Vietnam Women's Memorial, with a provocative sculpture, was added to the area in 1993.

On the other side of the Reflecting Pool is the newer Korean War Veterans Memorial featuring steel sculptures of nineteen battle-clad soldiers in ponchos and a Pool of Remembrance honoring those "who answered the call to defend a country they never knew and a people they never met." This memorial reminds visitors that more than 56,000 Americans lost their lives in Korea answering that "call."

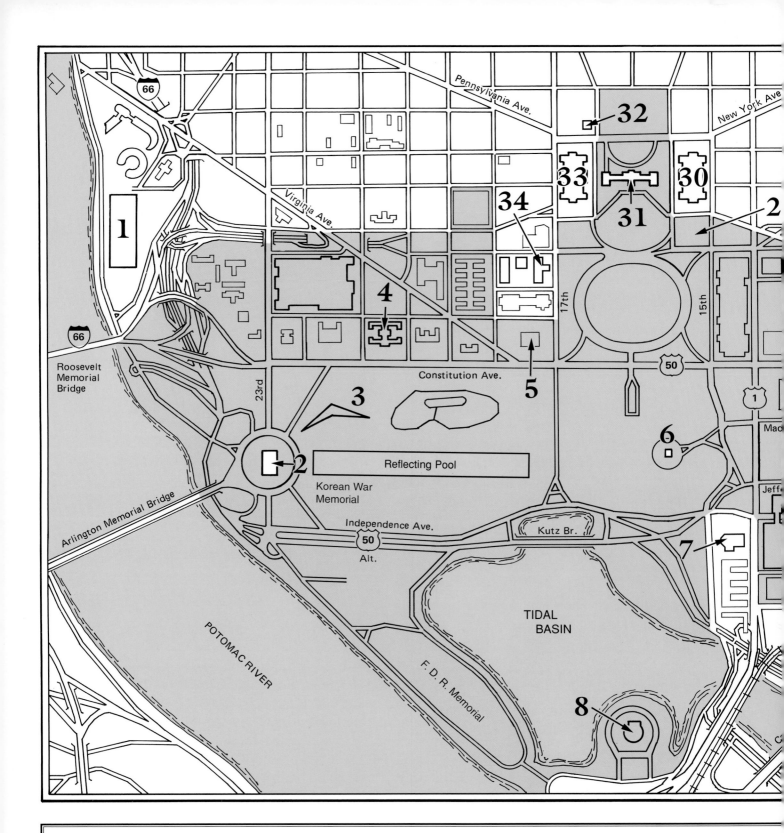

WALKING MAP OF THE MALL

1. John F. Kennedy Center
2. Lincoln Memorial
3. Vietnam Memorial
4. Federal Reserve Building
5. Organization of American States
6. Washington Monument

7. U.S. Holocaust Memorial Museum
8. Jefferson Memorial
9. Department of Agriculture
10. The Smithsonian
11. "The Castle" Smithsonian

12. Freer Gallery of Art
13. Arthur M. Sackler Gallery
14. Arts & Industries Building
15. National Air & Space Museum
16. U.S. Botanical Gardens
17. U.S. Capital

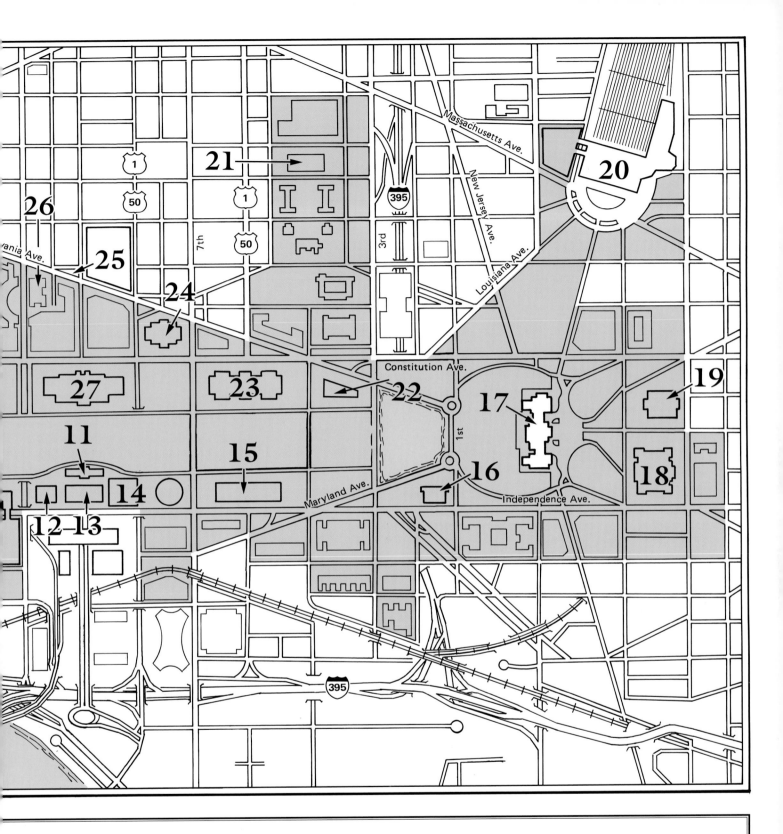

18. Library of Congress
19. Supreme Court Building
20. Union Station
21. National Building Museum
22. National Gallery East Wing
23. National Gallery of Art

24. National Archives
25. Pennsylvania Avenue
26. Old Post Office Building
27. National History Museum
28. National Museum of American
    History

29. Pershing Square
30. Treasury Department
31. The White House
32. Blair House
33. Executive Office Building
34. American Red Cross Building

Freer Art Gallery

Arts and Industries Building, Smithsonian Institution

National Gallery of Art

East Building, National Gallery of Art

The Chess Players, John Marshall Park

Old Post Office Building and statue of Benjamin Franklin

Albert Einstein Bronze, Constitution Avenue

Inside Kennedy Center

National Museum of American History

Department of Agriculture

Korean War Memorial

Organization of American States Building

The Wall of Names, Vietnam Veterans Memorial

Dumbarton Oaks

70

Pershing Square

National Zoological Park

Southwest Marina

The Jefferson Memorial, another good walk from a subway stop, is on the far side of the Tidal Basin. Like the Lincoln Memorial, it is particularly imposing at night. The 19-foot bronze statue of Jefferson stands under a simple rotunda in the center of this circular building with four open entrances. On the four walls are excerpts from four of Jefferson's most famous writings, including the Declaration of Independence. Take time to read them. They are as meaningful today as they were in the 18th century. This beautiful memorial was dedicated on the 200th anniversary of this brilliant man's birth, April 13, 1743.

Beside the Tidal Basin, not far from the Jefferson Memorial, is the city's newest major memorial, this one to Franklin D. Roosevelt, the nation's only President elected four times. The spaciousness of this seven-acre area of sculpture, stone and water adds to its appeal. There are two large sculptures of FDR, one with his dog Fala. The other— added in 2000 after considerable heated debate — shows the War II leader in a wheelchair (as he was not photographed by press photographers during his years as President, 1933-1945). There are also extremely impressive smaller sculptures of men in Depression bread lines, as well as one of a man listening closely to one of FDR's "fireside chats" on the radio. There is also a large sculpture of the memorably different and distinctive First Lady, Eleanor Roosevelt.

And don't miss the National Archives, part of the Federal Triangle between Pennsylvania and Constitution Avenues. Here you will find the Declaration of Independence (a single sheet of parchment), the Constitution of the United States (usually only the first and last four pages are displayed), and the Bill of Rights (notice the First Amendment appears as the Third amendment, because the states failed to ratify the first two proposed amendments). Helium fills the bronze and glass cases so the priceless documents are not in contact with air. When not on display, they are lowered into a fireproof and bombproof vault.

And at the Archives you can research your family's background or a specific part of American history, with staff to help you, including the Watergate tapes that led a House Judiciary Committee to vote for impeachment and a president to choose resignation instead.

Mount Vernon, George Washington's estate on the Potomac, is 16 miles south of Washington, about a half-hour by car or bus. From April until Labor Day, Mount Vernon can also be reached by boat. On some summer days, there are more than 10,000 visitors, so come early. Expect to spend about two hours to see the mansion (rooms seem small to the 20th century visitor), the grounds, the stables and other buildings on this 18th-century plantation. From the veranda, there is an unspoiled view of the Potomac, much as it was in Washington's time.

For those with a car, a drive north, to view Great Falls, where the Potomac crashes through rocks and drops more than 75 feet, is highly recommended. Great Falls is about seven miles from the D.C. line. And be sure to see this unforgettable scene from the Virginia side. You cannot see the Falls from the Maryland side now.

The 'Greatest Monstrosity'

There are dozens of other things to do and see in Washington. For example: please notice the Old Executive Office Building next to the White House. "The EOB" is maligned by many and praised by few, like me, who believe this building makes most modern architecture seem to be boring, dull, predictable, childish stuff. President Hoover was one of many prominent men who rapped it for the multiplicity of its architectural themes. It's said to be French Second Empire style, more or less. Called the world's largest office building when it was built at President Grant's order (the Pentagon is said to be the largest now), the EOB has 1,572 gabled windows. Once home for the Departments of State, War (later Army) and Navy, it has 10 acres of floor space and marble stairways with bronze balusters. After the State Department moved out, federal budget people moved in and it was closed to the public for nearly 40 years. Public tours are limited and require reservations.

In addition to the Office of Management and Budget, numerous White House people work here and this is where Ollie North and Fawn Hall had their "shredding party" in 1987. When an Eisenhower commission wanted to destroy this huge building, former President Harry Truman said: "I don't want it torn down. I think it's the greatest monstrosity in America!"

Arlington National Cemetery, on 612 acres, about half of which was once owned by Robert E. Lee, is the nation's most famous hallowed ground. More than 60,000 war dead plus 140,000 other servicemen and dependents are buried here. About 75 new graves are added each week.

The Tomb of the Unknown Soldier is guarded by soldiers of the Third Infantry's crack Honor Guard Company, a spit and polish outfit that takes part in about 18 funerals a day. This is the only active Army unit still using horses and nothing can replace them. Their continued presence seems as certain as death. A military funeral with full honors but without horses is unthinkable.

The changing of the guard ceremony, every hour on the hour beside the Unknown tombs, is surely memorable. On a hillside below the former Custis-Lee Mansion, now called Arlington House, are the graves of President Kennedy and his brother Robert. There is a fine view of the city from the mansion's portico.

The cemetery's Memorial Amphitheater is the site of Memorial Day and Veterans Day speeches. Beside the amphitheater is a small memorial, dedicated in 1987, to more than 60,000 Korean War dead and missing.

The Octagon House, two blocks from the White House at 18th and New York Avenue, is an interesting and historic place most tourists never visit. President and Mrs. Madison moved here after the British burned the White House in 1814. In the circular room above the entrance, James Madison ratified the treaty of Ghent.

The Corcoran Gallery of Art, a block from the Old EOB, concentrates on American art with paintings by Stuart, Copley, Peale, Cassatt, Homer, Sargent, Eakins, Ryder, Sloan, Bellows, and many others. There is also a good collection of Corot's landscapes. And the Corcoran Gallery is in the midst of a major expansion.

Next to the Corcoran is the Red Cross Headquarters with these words on the front

Old Stone House, Georgetown

Springtime in D.C.

of the building: "In memory of Heroic Women of the Civil War." And next to the Red Cross building, relative researchers can find the DAR Genealogical Library. There are many fascinating things to see in Washington and many places to study almost anything in Washington, too.

Including animals. The National Zoo, near Metro stop on Connecticut Avenue, is one of the nation's best zoos and unlike some other famous ones, it's free. Two expensive giant pandas from China, Mei Xiang and Tian-Tian, were added as the 21st century began and they have much specially designed outdoor space, complete with bamboo, just for them. This couple also has many human admirers of all ages. They line up to watch them.

Dupont Circle and Embassy Row

Visitors to Washington who don't mind walking might enjoy daytime strolls around some of the city's famous neighborhoods.

The Dupont Circle area is recommended for such a stroll and the Heurich House at 1307 New Hampshire Avenue, now home for the Columbia Historical Society, is a good place to start. You will see a fine Victorian home (built in 1892-94 for the city's most famous brewer, Christian Heurich, who lived to be 103 years old) and find excellent books on the city's history.

Check out other old mansions such as the James G. Blaine House at 20th and Massachusetts and the Walsh-McLean House at 2020 Massachusetts which cost $835,000 (unfurnished) when completed in 1903. Evalyn Walsh McLean, owner of the Hope Diamond (the Smithsonian has it now), lived here. It's now the Indonesian embassy. Many of the great mansions that made Dupont Circle the city's wealthiest neighborhood at the turn of the century have been razed, but enough remain to entice a visitor curious about Washington's past.

While in the Dupont Circle area, find time to visit one of the world's most delightful art museums, the Phillips, at 21st and Q Streets. Once a family home, it still seems more like a home than a museum. Relax in parlors and sitting rooms as you study paintings by Renoir, Degas, Daumier, Monet, Manet, Cezanne. Near the Phillips, on Massachusetts Avenue, is Anderson House, a must visit for anyone interested in early American military history. It is also one of the city's few palatial mansions opened to the public.

The Textile Museum on S Street near Dupont Circle has Oriental rugs, Navajo blankets, Peruvian weavings. Next door is the Woodrow Wilson House with lots of Wilson memorabilia. He liked games. His wife, who lived there until her death in 1961, had a Ouija board and took part in seances in hope of contacting her husband (transcripts on display in the sewing room).

For the ambitious walker, a tourist can reach nearly two dozen embassies by going along Massachusetts Avenue from Sheridan Circle, past Dupont Circle and toward Observatory Circle. Foreign flags make them easy to spot. There are many fine old mansions on "Embassy Row." The huge British Embassy with a statue of Winston Churchill out front — yes he holds a cigar and yes he is making his "V for victory" sign — is a long walk up Massachusetts.

Before reaching the British Embassy, a visit to the Islamic Center, on Massachusetts beside Rock Creek Park, will not be forgotten. Strikingly different to Western eyes on the outside, with a 160-foot minaret tower, it is lush on the inside with thick Persian carpets, ornate Turkish tiles on the walls, and the sweet smell of incense. Tourists are warned: No bare legs inside the mosque, and shoes must be removed. A Moslem call to prayer is chanted five times a day. The prayer leader's niche or mihrab in the mosque faces Mecca.

(Following pages) Winter in Rock Creek Park

Still More Places to See

Georgetown, which preceded the United States and officially became part of Washington in 1895, appeals to some visitors. Row houses here, such as the kind John Kennedy lived in before moving to the White House, sell for around $500,000 and up, way up, believe it or not. Some Georgetown homes (with no front lawns) that certainly do not look like million-dollar houses from the outside now sell for more than two million. (In contrast, larger middle-class homes in Chevy Chase or American University Park begin around $350,000 and much larger homes in Cleveland Park around $450,000. Truly expensive homes are found in Spring Valley and the Foxhall Road area.) Georgetown has some good restaurants and antique shops. On weekend nights the center of Georgetown, around Wisconsin Avenue and M Street, is woefully overcrowded with youngsters, many from the suburbs, looking for a good time. This infuriates residents who do not view their area as a proper playpen for teenagers.

Many prominent Washingtonians live in Georgetown and amidst the row houses are some superb homes on large estates, notably Evermay near Oak Hill Cemetery. Evermay has one of the finest formal gardens in the city but is seldom open to the public. Oak Hill, on the edge of Rock Creek Park, is a lovely, hilly, tree-sheltered place with flower beds, shrubs, and winding paths. Dean Acheson is one of the many Georgetowners buried here.

Georgetown is also where the C&O (Chesapeake and Ohio) Canal begins. In the summer you can take a 1½ mile trip aboard a mule-drawn canal boat. Now 22 miles long, the canal at one time went 184 miles west to Cumberland, Maryland.

The Washington Cathedral, also called the National Cathedral, towers over northwest Washington. Not far from Georgetown and close to Cleveland Park, on land 400 feet above the Potomac, this magnificent Gothic structure from a distance and from the sky seems to be higher than the Capitol or Washington Monument. It has a 301-foot central tower and rows of flying buttresses. Hand-carved gargoyles, each one different, guard the cathedral from evil and also spout rain away from walls and stained glass. It is incontestably one of the greatest cathedrals on earth. And there is a great view of the city from the tower.

The National Shrine of the Immaculate Conception, beside Catholic University in northeast Washington, is the largest Catholic church in the western hemisphere. Three thousand can be seated here, 9,000 accommodated. It has a distinctive blue dome, its bell tower is 329 feet high and it has the largest mosaic of Christ in the world (almost 4,000 square feet).

Also in northeast is the National Arboretum, magnificent in the spring when dogwoods and azaleas are blooming. It has nine miles of roads but the gardens can be enjoyed by walkers.

The Evening Parade on Friday nights at the Marine Barracks in southeast Washington is memorable but seating reservations are recommended. This is the oldest post of the Marine Corps and is where the commandant and the Marine Corps band are quartered. Fort McNair, in southwest Washington, is an interesting old Army post with a famed "General's Row" of homes backed by the Washington Channel of the Potomac.

In 1865, the four convicted of conspiracy in the assassination of Lincoln were hanged here (where tennis courts are now).

There are so many other places to see in Washington that a book of this size cannot begin to mention them all. But the Old Pension Building, on F Street between 4th and 5th Streets, is surely a sight to see. And don't just look at it from the outside. It's the enormous room inside, where a dozen inaugural balls have been held and where you will find the eight largest columns ever built in Roman style (25 feet in circumference at the base and with colossal Corinthian capitals about 80 feet from the floor) that won't be soon forgotten. The old building has been spruced up and now also houses the National Building Museum.

A few blocks away, beside two subway stops, are the National Museum of American Art and National Portrait Gallery, both in the old Patent Office Building at 8th and G Streets, the fourth oldest building in the city. The museum certainly does not receive the attention it deserves. It frequently has marvelous shows. An extensive one in 1996 of New York City's so-called "Ashcan School" of superb drawing and painting (early 20th century) was unforgettable. There is also a National Museum of Women in the Arts (downtown New York Avenue near 13th in what used to be a movie theater). As might be expected, there are paintings by Mary Cassatt and Georgia O'Keeffe.

Naturalists and the more adventurous should consider a visit to Theodore Roosevelt Island Park, 91 acres of marsh, swamp, and forest in the Potomac River between the Key and Roosevelt bridges. It's one of the least visited memorials in the city, with a 17-foot high statue of Teddy Roosevelt. You get there by footbridge high above the Potomac. And while exploring the island, it's wise to stay on the trails. This way you avoid the island's plentiful crop of poison ivy and stinging nettle.

Inside National Building Museum

Memorial Bridge and Potomac River

Even a cursory essay on Washington would be incomplete without mention of all the outdoor sculpture. And it's not just military men on horseback. You will find all kinds of other subject matter in bronze, marble, stone and concrete. Buffaloes and lions guard bridges. There are Masonic sphinxes, Balinese demons, wrestling bears, eagles, angels, and sea nymphs. Among the many people not on horseback are Ben Franklin, Alexander Hamilton, Nathan Hale, St. Bernadette, John Wesley, Edmund Burke, Einstein and Army nurse Jane Delano. And there are countless other heroes (let's not forget the Iwo Jima monument near Arlington Cemetery) and heroines (the Mary McLeod Bethune bronze in Lincoln Park is delightful). There are even bronze chess players in recently developed John Marshall Park, which replaced a needless street off Pennsylvania Avenue. Those who play chess can try to figure out the next move. Let it be known the game is soon to end.

There are outdoor sculptures that depict love, justice, faith, law, peace, serenity, and sacrifice. A magnificent statue by Augustus Saint-Gaudens known as "Grief" (after Mark Twain said it embodied all human grief) is in Rock Creek Cemetery. It was created at the request of historian Henry Adams as memorial to his beloved wife, an invalid who committed suicide. The seated six-foot figure, neither male nor female, wears a full-length cloak with a hood that deeply shadows the face.

Visitors will discover their own favorite pieces among the more than 500 outdoor sculptures in Washington. Indeed, they will discover their own favorite places in this city that offers something exciting and meaningful to everyone.

A final thought: Despite the beauty of the city in the spring, some of us believe that the loveliest time of year in Washington is fall. If you can arrange to visit the nation's capital in autumn, do so. Not only beautiful but far less crowded.

Tragically the events of September 11, 2001 have drastically altered many of the attractions, not just here in Washington, D.C., but in virtually every other city in the world. Buildings and monuments that for centuries have been open to the public have now been closed. Many beautiful thoroughfares are now barricaded as the world shifts to a state of heightened security.

No one can predict what form this will take or what the eventual outcome will be. Washington, D.C. is no exception. It is, as they say, "a work in progress." Good judgement would now dictate checking ahead to make sure the visitation you desire is open and available.

I love my hometown, Washington, D.C., and millions of visitors must, too, because they keep coming back.

— TOM SCANLAN.

About the Photographer

Mae Scanlan, a free lance and stock photographer specializing in scenic photography, has lived in Washington since 1948. Her photos have appeared in magazines, newspapers, books, calendars, brochures, trade publications and on posters. She has published much humorous verse, including close to 1,000 limericks, and is currently working on a photo book about New England, as well as one on cats.

About the Author

Tom Scanlan has lived in Washington since 1928. He wrote more than 1,000 columns of opinion during his 37 years of newspaper work, which included 11 years as editor of *Federal Times*. His writings on jazz music include a 56-program history of jazz for the Voice of America and two books, *Rhythm Man* (with guitarist Steve Jordan) and *The Joy of Jazz*, a memoir of the swing era. He is currently working on a lengthy study of jazz criticism dating from the early 1930s. In 2001 he became a "Golden Owl" (denoting 50 years of active membership) of the National Press Club.

Tom and Mae Scanlan, now grandparents, have been married since 1954.

Washington Monument